MW01688257

CLIVEDEN PRESS

Copyright © 1990 by Cliveden Press.
All rights reserved.
Published by Cliveden Press,
An Egmont Company, Egmont House,
P.O. Box 111, Great Ducie Street,
Manchester M60 3BL.
Printed in Czechoslovakia.
ISBN 0 7235 4331 3

HANS CHRISTIAN ANDERSEN

The Little Mermaid

and other Fairy Tales

Contents

Retold by
Brenda Apsley

Illustrated by
Annabel Spenceley

Quite True

It was evening, and in a certain hen-house, as the sun went down the hens flew up to roost. One of them, a very respectable white hen who always laid her eggs regularly and behaved well, preened her feathers. As she preened with her beak a tiny white feather fluttered to the ground. "Never mind," said the white hen with a laugh, "for the more I preen myself, the more handsome I become."

Soon the sensible white hen fell asleep, and in the henhouse where hen lay close to hen only an occasional rustle of feathers could be heard as they settled comfortably in their sleep.

But one of the hens could not sleep that night. Over and over again she thought of what the white hen had said: "The more I preen myself, the more handsome I become."

At last she could remain silent no longer, and roused her neighbour. "Did you hear what I heard a while ago?" she whispered. "I will not mention names, but there is a hen in this very henhouse who intends to pluck out all her feathers to make herself more beautiful. Have you ever heard such a thing? If I were the cock I would be angry."

The hen's words were overheard by a family of owls who lived in a tree beside the henhouse. "Whatever next?" said Mother Owl. "I never thought I'd see the day when a hen should be so silly."

Mother Owl flew to the dovecote nearby. *"Tu-whit, tu-whoo,"* she hooted. "Have you heard? One of the hens has plucked out all her feathers, just to please the cock. She must be freezing to death, if she is not dead already."

"Where? Where?" cooed the doves.

"In the farm over there," the owl replied. "Why, I've as good as seen the sight myself. It's a terrible story, but quite true."

"True! True!" cooed the doves. "Every word is true, true!"

The doves told the tale in the poultry yard. "There is a hen, or it might be two hens, who have plucked out all their feathers so that they'll attract the cock's attention. Such a foolish thing to do in this cold weather. Indeed they are dead already!"

The cock in the poultry yard heard the tale. "Wake up! Wake up!" he crowed. "Three hens have died of love for a cock. They stripped all their feathers off, stupid things!"

"Oh, what a scandal!" shrieked the bats. "Let it be known as a warning to everyone."

"Yes, let it be known," clucked the hens.

"Let it be known," crowed the cock.

So the story was told and re-told until at last it was carried back to the henhouse where it had started. "There are five hens who plucked out all their feathers for love of a cock," the story ran. "Crazy with jealousy, they pecked each other, and now all five are dead!"

The white hen who had lost one tiny feather was shocked. "How disgraceful!" she said. "Such silly creatures!"

And the story is still told today, and respectable hens still cluck over their companions' behaviour. But one thing *is* quite true – one little feather may grow into five hens!

The Emperor's New Clothes

Many years ago there lived an emperor who was so fond of clothes that he spent all his time and money dressing up. He didn't care about his army, he didn't care about the theatre, and he only drove out in his carriage to show off his new clothes. He had a different coat for every hour of the day, and as for matters of state – he was more often to be found in his dressing room than in the council chambers.

One day a pair of shady characters arrived in the city. They claimed to be weavers – very special weavers. They claimed that the cloth they wove was not only very beautiful, but also had great magical properties. Even when it was made up into clothes their cloth was invisible to anyone who was either unfit for his job or very, very stupid.

"Wonderful!" said the emperor when he heard about the magical cloth. "Now I'll be able to discover which men in my kingdom are fit for the jobs they hold, and which are stupid. I'll know which are the wise men – and which are the fools. I must have some clothes made from the magical cloth." And the emperor gave the two rogues a large sum of money so that they could get started right away.

The imposters set up two looms and acted as if they were working hard, but of course the looms were empty. Before long they asked for fine coloured silks and pure gold thread to weave into the cloth – but the silks and gold thread went into their own pockets!

After a while the emperor wanted to know how the weavers were getting on. But when he remembered that anyone who was stupid or unfit for his job would not be able to see the cloth, he felt rather awkward about going himself. He decided that it might be better to send someone else for a start. "I know, I'll send my honest old minister," the emperor decided. "He's very sensible, and no one can say he's unfit for his job."

So the old minister went to see the weavers at their looms. Dear me! he thought. I can't see anything! But he kept his thoughts to himself.

The imposters asked the minister to step closer. Did he not think the patterns beautiful, the colours a delight?

The old minister peered closer, but could see nothing (for the simple reason that there was nothing to see!) Am I really stupid? he thought.

Am I really unfit for my job?

"Well, do you like the cloth?" asked one of the weavers. "You haven't said a word."

The old minister decided to pretend that he could see the cloth. "The cloth is charming," he said, "quite beautiful. The design, the pattern, yes, I will tell the emperor that they are quite – remarkable."

"We are glad to hear it," said the imposters, who then demanded more silks, gold thread and money so that they could finish the cloth. The silks and money went into their own pockets, of course.

Soon after, the emperor sent another official to inspect the cloth. He looked, saw nothing on the looms, but didn't dare say so, for fear of appearing stupid and unfit for his position.

"Isn't the fabric lovely?" asked the imposters, pointing out a pattern that didn't exist.

The official didn't want to be thought stupid, so he made admiring noises about the cloth, and then reported to the emperor. "The cloth is magnificent," he said.

News of the magical cloth soon spread around the city, and it wasn't long before the emperor himself decided to look at the cloth. He went to the weaving rooms with many attendants, and saw the cheats busy at the empty looms.

"Look at the splendid cloth, your majesty!" said the old minister. "Such patterns!"

"And the wonderful colours!" said the official, for he was sure that everyone else could see the magical cloth.

This is terrible, thought the emperor. I can't see a thing! Am I stupid? Unfit to be emperor? I can't admit that I can't see anything!

So the emperor fingered the imaginary cloth. "The cloth is charming,"

he said. "It has my highest approval."

All the other attendants stared in surprise. They couldn't see a single thread – but they couldn't admit it, so they echoed the emperor's words. "Charming! Quite charming!" they said. "So unusual!" And they advised the emperor to have the cloth made up into a new set of royal robes that he

could wear at a great procession that was to take place soon. The emperor agreed.

On the night before the procession the two cheats were still busy in the weaving rooms, pretending to cut, stitch and trim the imaginary cloth. Dozens of candles flickered around them as they worked, and it wasn't until dawn was breaking that they at last announced: "The clothes are ready!"

The emperor came to look at the clothes. "Here are the trousers," said the imposters, "and the jacket, and the cloak. They are as light as cob-webs. You would think that you were wearing nothing at all – but that, of course, is the beauty of the cloth."

"Yes, indeed," agreed the emperor's attendants, though they could see nothing.

"If you will take off your clothes," said one of the cheats to the emperor, "we will dress you in your new robes here in front of the mirror."

The emperor took off all his clothes and the cheats pretended to hand him the new ones, one item at a time.

The emperor turned and twisted in front of the mirror.

"How elegant!" the attendants said. "How well the clothes fit! What splendid colours! Such rich material!"

Just then a servant entered. "The royal canopy is at the head of the procession," he said, "if your majesty is ready."

"I'm ready," said the emperor, and he turned once more in front of the mirror. "The clothes really are an excellent fit, don't you think?"

The courtiers who were to carry his train stooped as if to pick it up, for they were not going to let anyone know that they couldn't see anything.

So the emperor took his place under the rich velvet canopy, and trumpets blew to announce the start of the royal procession.

A huge crowd lined the route and they stared when they saw the emperor, but they didn't dare admit that they couldn't see any clothes. "Doesn't the emperor look magnificent!" they cried. "Such elegant new clothes!"

Only one person in the whole crowd dared to speak the truth. A little boy looked at the emperor and started to laugh. "He's got nothing on!" the boy cried. "The emperor's wearing his birthday suit!"

His laughter was infectious, and before very long the whole crowd laughed and pointed at the emperor. "He's got nothing on!" they cried.

The emperor realised that they were right. He felt very foolish, and vowed that never again would he pretend to see what was not there.

And the two rogues who had tricked him? As the emperor's procession moved on they rode out through the city gates, their saddlebags filled with silks and gold. And *they* laughed loudest of all...

The Shepherdess and the Chimney Sweep

Have you ever seen a very old wooden cabinet, black with age and carved all over with flowers and leaves?

Once such a chest stood in a sitting-room; it had once belonged to the family's great great grandmother. It was covered from top to bottom with carved roses, tulips and other flowers, and the heads and antlers of small deer.

In the middle of the cabinet was the figure of a man – or something like a man. He was not a handsome figure, for he had the legs of a goat, a long curly beard, and sticking out from his forehead were short horns. He was always grinning; you could hardly call his expression a smile.

The children of the house called the figure the Goatsleg-High-Adjutant-Sergeant-Major-General, for they thought such a strange fellow deserved a strange name.

All the time his eyes were turned to a small table under a mirror, where a small china shepherdess stood. On her dress was pinned a tiny china rose, and her wide straw bonnet was tied with a pale pink ribbon. Her shoes were of gilt, and in her hand she held a shepherd's crook.

Beside her stood another china figure – a chimney sweep dressed all in black. Though his clothes were black there was not a trace of soot on his hands and face. Beside him stood brushes and a ladder.

The shepherdess and the chimney sweep had stood side by side for a long time. Both were young, each as fragile and pretty as the other, and

they had become engaged, so well suited were they.

Another figure stood on the same table – but he was very different. He was a Chinese mandarin who could nod his head, and he said that he was the shepherdess's grandfather and guardian.

When one day the Goatsleg-High-Adjutant-Sergeant-Major-General asked if he could marry the shepherdess, the mandarin nodded his head in agreement. "He will make you an excellent husband," he told the shepherdess. "I think he's made of mahogany, and his cabinet is full of silver. And I believe he has many valuable things in his secret drawers."

"But I don't want to go into that dark cupboard," said the shepherdess, "for I've heard that he has eleven china wives in there already."

"Then you can be the twelfth," said the mandarin. "The marriage will take place soon... this very night, I think." And his head nodded until he was fast asleep.

The shepherdess started to cry, and spoke to her beloved sweep. "I must ask you to come out into the wide

world with me," she said, "for we cannot stay here."

"Your will is my will," the sweep replied. "There are many chimneys to sweep, so I will earn money for us. Let us start at once."

The chimney sweep climbed down from the table, and helped the shepherdess to make her way down, with the help of his ladder. But when they were on the floor they heard the most awful noises coming from the black cabinet, and they looked up to see the Goatsleg-High-Adjutant-Sergeant-Major-General jumping up and down with rage shouting, "They're running away! They're running away!"

The shepherdess and the chimney sweep hid in a cupboard under the windowseat. A play was being acted in a toy theatre there, and in the audience sat playing cards, the queens of hearts, clubs, spades and diamonds fanning themselves on the front row while the knaves stood behind. The play was about two lovers who could not marry, and the shepherdess started to cry as she watched. "It is my own story," she cried. "I cannot bear to watch. I must get away."

But when they went outside they saw the Chinese mandarin, and he was shaking with rage. "Let's hide," said the sweep.

"It's no use," said the shepherdess, "for no one will help us. They are afraid of the mandarin. We must go out into the wide world."

"But have you thought how large and lonely a place it is?" asked the sweep. "That we can never come back here again?"

"Yes," said the china shepherdess, "and still we must go."

"The only path I know lies through the chimney," the sweep said. "We must go through the stove, then up the flue, and right up the chimney. We shall climb so high that no one will reach us, and right at the top we'll find a hole that will lead into the wide world."

The sweep led the shepherdess through the stove, through the flue, and up the chimney, where it was black as night. "Look up," said the sweep. "The loveliest star is shining above us."

It was a real star shining down as if to show them the way and, slowly, they climbed up and up, higher and higher, until at last they came to the edge of the chimney pot. There they sat down to rest.

Above them stretched the dark night sky with all its stars, and below lay the town with all its roofs. They were sitting on top of the wide world – and the shepherdess was frightened. "The world is too large," she wept. "I cannot bear it! Oh, if only I were back on the table under the mirror. I shall never be happy here. If you love me, please take me back."

The chimney sweep reminded her of the mandarin and the Goatsleg-High-Adjutant-Sergeant-Major-General, but nothing could persuade her not to go back.

So they made the long journey down the chimney again, down the flue and through the stove. Everything seemed quiet – but in the middle of the floor lay the old Chinese mandarin. Trying to follow them, he had fallen from the table, and now lay broken in three pieces. His head had rolled into a corner.

"This is terrible," said the china shepherdess. "I shall never get over it. It is all my fault."

The sweep told her not to worry. "He'll be glued together, and if they put a rivet through his neck he'll be just as he always was."

The chimney sweep was right. The old Chinaman was mended, and

stood beside the shepherdess and the chimney sweep, as he had always done – but he could no longer nod his head.

"Well, now that things are back to normal, do I still have permission to marry your grand-daughter?" asked the Goatsleg-High-Adjutant-Sergeant-Major-General.

The shepherdess and the sweep looked towards the Chinaman – but he could no longer nod his head. So the two china lovers stood beside each other on the table just as they had always done, until the day they were broken.

The Fir Tree

In a clearing in the middle of a dark wood stood a young fir tree. He was a fine tree, and had a fine place in the wood, where the sun warmed his branches and gentle breezes rustled his green foliage.

But the young fir tree was not happy. "Why am I smaller than the other trees?" the tree asked. "When will I have thick foliage like my older brothers?"

"What, you don't like being young?" a very old tree asked. "How strange!"

"It's not strange," the little fir tree said. "I want to stretch my branches far around. I want the birds to build their nests in my branches."

Every year the woodcutters went into the wood to cut down some of the older trees, but of course they didn't cut down the little fir tree. "I am good for nothing," the tree whined. "Nobody takes any notice of me. Why don't the woodcutters cut me down? Perhaps I could be a tall mast on a sailing ship then, and see the world."

"What foolishness," said the sun. "Be happy where you are. Enjoy your youth." But still the little fir tree complained...

Just before Christmas woodcutters again went into the wood, and this time they cut down smaller trees, just like the little fir tree. They carried them off on carts, still with their branches

intact. "Where are they taking those trees?" the little fir tree asked.

It was the sparrows who told him. "The trees are taken into houses in the town," they said. "They are decorated with golden balls and coloured ribbons."

"And then?" asked the fir tree. "What happens then?"

"That we do not know," said the sparrows. "All we know is that the trees look very beautiful."

"Then I must make sure I am taken away next year," the fir tree decided. "Going to the town will be even better than going to sea."

"Be happy where you are," the wind advised. "Enjoy your youth."

But the little fir tree would not listen.

When the woodcutters went into the wood one year later, the little fir tree had grown into a beautiful shape, and he was the first to be cut down. Though he had wanted to be cut down, the little fir tree felt sad to leave the wood, but he began to feel better when he was carried into the town and unpacked.

The fir tree found himself in the royal palace! He was put into a tub of sand, and the princess and her ladies-in-waiting decorated his branches. They hung coloured balls and baskets filled with sweets on the fir tree, and fixed hundreds of tiny candles among his branches. At the top they added a large star made of gold tinsel.

That night there was a great party at the royal palace, and all the visitors stopped as they came in to admire the little fir tree. The candles were lit, and

when they had burned down, the children were allowed to take the balls and sweet baskets from the tree. The tree was so happy. "I can't wait for tomorrow," he said as the party ended. "I wonder what decorations they will hang from my branches then?"

But the next morning the servants carried the fir tree out of the great hall and upstairs to a dark loft. There they left him, without light or fresh air.

The fir tree was very lonely, and thought of his home in the wood. The snow would be lying white and crisp on the ground now, and the fresh wind would be hurrying through the trees.

"Hello," a tiny mouse said. "How are you, old fir tree?"

"Old?" said the fir tree. "I am not old!"

"Very well," said the mouse. "Tell me where you come from."

The fir tree told the mouse about the wood; how the sun shone on his branches, and how the birds sang all day long. Then he told of the Christmas party, and how he had been decorated by the princess. "Look," he said, "my shiny gold star is still in place."

When the mouse ran off the fir tree was alone again – and he stayed that way for many months, until one day the door of the loft opened and he was dragged down the stairs.

The fir tree was thrown into a corner of the stable yard, but he was happy. He could smell new-mown grass, and he could feel the sun on his branches. He tried to spread them out to catch some warmth, but he could not! His branches were dry and yellow, his bark cracked and dusty.

As he saw a servant coming towards him with a large saw, the fir tree realised that he was to be cut up for firewood. "It is over now," said the tree, thinking back to his time in the tree, thinking back to his time in the beautiful wood. "Oh, how I wish I had enjoyed myself when I could. I should have been happy where I was."

The Little Mermaid

Far, far out in the deepest oceans the sea is a deep cornflower blue, and as clear as glass. The water is deep, deeper than any anchor has ever sunk, and it is here that the people of the sea live.

In the bare white sand grow wonderful plants and trees that sway to and fro in the water, and fishes large and small swim among their branches.

In the deepest part of this underwater garden stands the palace of the sea king. Its walls are made of coral, its long narrow windows of amber, and the roof is made of oyster shells which open and close with the movement of the water. Inside each oyster shell gleams a shining pearl.

At the time of our story the sea king had been a widower for some years, and his old mother kept house for him. She was a wise old lady, though very proud of her royal rank and position. She was especially proud of her six grand-daughters, and thought them the most beautiful mermaids in the whole ocean.

All six were indeed beautiful, but the youngest was the loveliest of all. Her skin was as soft as the palest rose petal, her eyes deep sapphire blue, and her voice was so sweet that when she sang all the fish gathered to listen. But, like all mermaids, she had no legs, her body ending in a fish's tail.

Around the palace was a large garden where strange plants and trees grew, lit by the sun that filtered down through the water. Each mermaid princess had a plot in the garden, one planted in the shape of a whale, another like a mermaid. But the youngest mermaid's plot was always the same: it was shaped like the sun, and in it she planted only flowers that were the colour of the sun.

The little mermaid was quiet and thoughtful. While her sisters wore silks and jewels they had found in wrecks on the seabed, she asked only for a white statue of a boy, which she put in her garden beside a red tree like a weeping willow.

Nothing pleased the mermaid more than to hear of the world above the seas. She never tired of hearing her grandmother's tales of ships and cities, men and animals, flowers and birds . . . and she longed to see them for herself.

"You may see them when you are fifteen," her grandmother told her. "Then you can swim to the surface of the sea and look at ships. You can even swim into the harbour and watch the people that live there."

One by one, as they reached the age of fifteen, the mermaid princesses were allowed to swim to the surface,

and each returned with wonderful stories of life on land. They told of houses and people, of lights twinkling in windows like stars, of churches with tall spires, of birds singing. The five older princesses would swim to the surface together each evening, leaving the little mermaid alone, gazing after them.

And then at last the little mermaid was fifteen.

She left her home on the seabed and floated up to the surface. The sun had just set, and stars shone in the deep blue sky. The sea was still and calm, and upon it sat a tall, three-masted ship. Music and laughter drifted from the ship on the still air, and hundreds of lanterns lit its decks.

The little mermaid swam up to a porthole. Inside were finely-dressed young men, celebrating the birthday of a handsome prince. When he went on deck to greet his crew hundreds of

fireworks were released, and the mermaid watched, entranced. She had never seen anything so wonderful.

As the party came to an end and the lanterns were put out, still the little mermaid watched.

But as she watched there came a rumbling and a murmuring deep in the sea. Black clouds rolled across the sky, and distant thunder sounded. Lightning flashes cracked across the sky, and the tall ship was tossed like a

toy between the huge waves that sprang up.

The ship's mast snapped, it keeled on its side, and a great black wave washed over it, sweeping the crew into the sea.

In the light from a flash of lightning the little mermaid saw the prince, and swam towards him. She held his head above the water, and let the raging sea carry them where it liked.

When morning came the storm was spent, but the ship was nowhere to be seen. The prince lay lifeless, his face pale and his eyes closed. Please let him live, thought the little mermaid.

Suddenly the mermaid saw dry land ahead, and she swam towards it. She laid the prince on the warm sand at the water's edge, and hid behind some rocks to see if he would be rescued.

Soon a young girl appeared. She brought help, and the prince was revived. He smiled at the people around him, and thanked them for rescuing him, for he remembered nothing of the little mermaid. When he walked away from the sea the little mermaid dived under the water and swam to her home in the palace.

Her sisters asked what she had seen on her visit to the surface, but she refused to tell them.

The little mermaid found out where the prince's kingdom lay, and every evening she would swim towards it. She floated beside his palace and watched as he ate, danced and sang.

She longed to leave the sea and live on land – then she could be closer than ever to her prince.

"Why can't I live on the land?" she asked her grandmother.

"Because you have a tail instead of legs," said the old mermaid. "Men cannot live under the water as we can, and we cannot live on the land. Be happy as you are. Don't wish for something that cannot be."

But the little mermaid could not forget the prince, and she was determined to live on the land and win his love. "I will go to see the old sea witch," she decided. "She frightens me, but she may be able to tell me what to do."

The sea witch lived beyond the roaring whirlpools, where no flowers or plants grew, and no fish dared to swim. The witch's house was almost hidden in an eerie forest of creatures that were half animal and half plant. They looked like many-headed snakes growing out of the earth, and everything they touched they caught and held.

When she saw the forest the little mermaid almost turned back, but she thought of her prince and decided to go on. She tied her long hair close to her head, wrapped her arms around her body, and darted as quickly as she could through the clinging tentacles.

Fat water snakes swam around in a clearing in the forest, and there stood the sea witch's house, made from the remains of wrecked ships.

The old, ugly sea witch seemed to have been expecting the little mermaid. "I know why you are here," she said. "And I know what you want. You want legs instead of your tail so that the prince will fall in love with you. It is a foolish request, but I will grant it. Here is a potion I have prepared. Before the sun rises you must swim to the land and drink it. As your tail divides into the things men call legs you will feel terrible pain, and even though you will move beautifully, every step will be like walking on knives. Can you endure this? Decide, foolish child, before I grant your wish."

"I am willing!" the mermaid replied.

"There is something else you must know," the sea witch continued. "Once you take a human shape you can never again be a mermaid. You will never swim in the ocean again, or see your family. And if you fail to win the prince's love and he marries another, you will turn to foam on the water."

"Still I am willing," said the mermaid.

"So be it," said the sea witch. "Now we must talk of payment. My potion is costly – it will cost you your beautiful voice."

"But how shall I win the prince without my voice?" the mermaid asked.

"You will have your graceful body and your beautiful face," said the sea witch. "Now, do you still want the potion?"

The little mermaid nodded, and from that moment she was dumb, unable to sing or speak. She took the potion and swam away from the sea witch's house, past the palace to which she could never return, and up through the clear waters to the land.

Beside the prince's palace she drank the potion, and felt a pain so severe that she fainted and lay lifeless by the shore.

When she opened her eyes she saw the prince standing over her. Glancing down, she noticed that her fish's tail had disappeared – she now had legs!

"Where are you from?" asked the prince.

But the little mermaid could only smile in reply, and her eyes were so sad that the prince took her into his palace. Every step she took was agony, yet she endured it gladly. She was with the prince at last.

The little mermaid was given fine clothes to wear, and when the prince

and his court gathered in the great hall she danced for him. The prince was delighted, and called her his little foundling. "If only I could sing for him, too," the little mermaid thought. But she could not – she had given her voice to the old sea witch.

As each day passed the prince grew fonder of the little mermaid. He loved her as one would a dear child, but the idea of marrying her and making her his queen never entered his head.

Do you not love me? the little mermaid's eyes seemed to say.

"Of course," the prince replied. "You are dearest of all to me, and you remind me of a beautiful girl I once saw. I was shipwrecked and thrown onto a foreign shore. A young girl saved my life. I would marry her but I doubt that I will ever find her again."

The little mermaid longed to cry out, "I was the one who saved your life! I carried you to the safety of the beach!" But of course she could not utter a sound.

Some time later the little mermaid heard a rumour that the prince was to be married to the daughter of a neighbouring king. She was not worried, for the prince had spoken to her about it. "I have to go and meet

this princess to please my mother and father," he said, "but I cannot love a stranger. If I must take a bride, it will be you, my little foundling."

So the prince and the little mermaid travelled on a fine ship to the neighbouring king's fine city.

When the prince met the princess he cried out in surprise. "It is you!" he said. "You are the one who saved me when I lay almost dead on the shore! I never thought I would see you again!" And of course he agreed to the marriage that had been arranged between them.

The little mermaid was happy for the prince, but sad for herself. On the prince's marriage she would turn into a wisp of sea foam. . .

The wedding ceremony was a marvellous occasion, and that night the prince and his bride set sail for his own country. There was music and dancing on board, and the little mermaid danced as she had never danced before. Though her feet hurt with every step she hardly felt the pain, so intense was the pain in her heart.

When the party was over and the

ship was quiet, the little mermaid leaned on the rails of the ship, gazing at the calm sea. As she watched, her sisters swam up to the ship! Their beautiful long hair had been cut off!

"We gave our hair to the sea witch to help you," they told her. "Before sunrise you must plunge this knife into the prince's heart and you will be saved. Your tail will grow again and you will be able to come and live under the sea again."

The little mermaid took the knife and went to the prince's bedside. But she could not kill him, and she flung the knife into the sea. Then she threw herself from the ship, and her body dissolved into soft white sea foam.

The little mermaid had no feeling of death. She could still see the morning sun and, floating above her, hundreds of lovely transparent figures. They floated through the air without wings – and the mermaid saw that she had become like them, and was rising above the waves. "Where am I going?" she asked.

"You are coming with us, the spirits of the air," the figures replied. "We fly to warm countries and bring cooling breezes to the people there. We spread the scent of flowers all over the earth, and try and do good whenever we can. By your suffering you have earned a place with us."

Looking down, the little mermaid saw that the prince was looking for her. He gazed at the sea as if he knew she had thrown herself into its depths.

"Let us away," whispered one of the spirits of the air. "There is work to be done."

With a final glance at the prince, the little mermaid soared into the air, and soon the ship was far behind. . .

The Brave Tin Soldier

There were once twenty-five tin soldiers, all of them brothers, for they had all been made from the same kitchen spoon. They were all exactly alike, in smart red and blue uniforms – all except one, who had only one leg. He had been the last to be made, and there just wasn't enough tin left for his second leg.

But the boy who got the tin soldiers as a birthday gift didn't mind – the one-legged soldier stood just as proud and straight as all the others.

The tin soldiers stood on a large table with lots of other toys, one of which was a castle made of cardboard. You could look through its tiny windows into real rooms, and outside a piece of mirror had been made to look like a lake, with model trees around it. But the prettiest thing about the castle – or so the brave tin soldier thought – was a little dancer who stood by the castle door. She wore a skirt of fine muslin, and a sash of blue ribbon across her shoulder, pinned in place by a gold tinsel rose. One of her legs was raised so high that the tin soldier could not see it, and he thought she had only one leg, as he did.

"She is beautiful," the tin soldier said. "She would be just the right wife for me, but I don't suppose she'd look twice at me. She lives in a splendid castle, and I share a cardboard box with twenty-four other soldiers!"

After supper the little boy put his toys away. He packed his tin soldiers into their box, but left the one-legged soldier out. "You can guard the castle," said the boy.

That pleased the tin soldier, and for the next few hours, while all the other toys played, he stood to attention, gazing at the dancer. The tin soldier and the dancer were the only toys that did not move.

As the clock struck midnight the lid flew off the jack-in-the-box, and an angry face popped out. "Hey, tin soldier!" cried the jack. "Keep your eyes to yourself! Stop staring at the pretty dancer!"

The tin soldier pretended not to hear, and carried on staring at the dancer.

"You won't do as I say, eh?" cried the jack angrily. "Just wait until tomorrow then. Just wait!"

The next morning the little boy put the tin soldier on the windowledge, and a sharp gust of wind – or was it the jack-in-the-box? – blew him out of the open window. Down, down, down he fell until he landed upside-down, his bayonet stuck between two paving stones.

Soon drops of rain began to fall, and the rain got heavier and heavier until the gutters ran with water.

"Look, here's a tin soldier," said a passing boy to his friend. "Let's make a paper boat for him and send him sailing!"

The tin soldier was tossed and bumped as his newspaper boat bobbed along the gutter, but still he stood tall and erect like a tiny guardsman.

Suddenly the boat dropped into a dark drain and a large rat raised its head from the water. "No entry without a passport!" the rat said. "Stop!"

The tin soldier said not a word, but still stood tall and erect. The rat tried to catch up with the paper boat, but the water ran faster, and the rat was soon left behind. The tin soldier breathed a small sigh of relief.

Up ahead the tin soldier could see daylight, and soon found himself in roaring, swirling, rushing waters. He was floating along a deep canal, and soon his fragile paper boat began to crumple.

Slowly the boat filled with water,

but still the tin soldier stood stiff and straight – even when the water covered his foot, then his chest, then his shoulders! Perhaps the dancer would be proud of me if she could see how bravely I am facing death, he thought.

Seconds later the paper boat fell apart and the tin soldier sank down, down under the water – and was immediately swallowed by a large fish! The tin soldier lay quite still as the fish swam slowly down the canal, but suddenly he was jolted around as the fish wriggled and squirmed, then lay quite still. What was happening?

The tin soldier soon found out, for a couple of hours later a sharp knife flashed by his arm, and he was lifted out of the dark fish and into the daylight. "Bless my soul," said a loud voice. "It's the one-legged tin soldier!"

The fish had been caught, sent to market, and bought by the cook in the house where the little boy lived!

Soon the tin soldier was back in the nursery with his young owner, and once again stood on guard outside the castle, gazing at the dancer who still stood balanced on one leg.

A little later a boy came to play in the nursery, and when he saw the one-legged tin soldier he laughed, and threw him onto the blazing fire! Perhaps he was jealous of his friend's toys, or perhaps the jack-in-the-box had put him up to it?

Whatever the reason, the brave tin soldier stood tall and straight as the flames licked around him and he slowly started to melt away. Even as he was melting he looked at the pretty dancer – and she seemed to be looking back at him.

The door of the room was opened, a gust of wind blew in, and the little dancer was wafted into the fire. For a few seconds she stood beside the tin soldier, then she vanished in the flames.

In the morning when the maid was clearing the ashes from the fire she found all that remained of the brave tin soldier – a tiny tin heart. And what do you think was beside it? The tinsel rose that was pinned to the little dancer's dress . . .

Thumbelina

Many years ago there lived a widow who had no children. One day she met a witch and spoke to her. "I would like to have a little child," the woman said. "Can you help me?"

"Of course," said the witch. "Take this seed and plant it in a flowerpot, and wait and see what happens!"

The widow did as the witch told her, and before long a lovely flower grew from the seed. When the flower's petals uncurled there stood a little girl! She was tiny, no bigger than the widow's thumb, so she called her Thumbelina.

The widow made Thumbelina a little bed from a walnut shell, with rose petals for blankets and a piece of thistledown for a pillow. During the day the tiny girl played on the table, where the widow had put a bowl of water with flowers around the edge. Thumbelina would row across the water on a tulip petal, singing sweetly.

One night, as the widow and Thumbelina lay sleeping, a toad

hopped in through an open window. "She'll make a fine wife for my son," said the toad, and he took the walnut-shell bed – and Thumbelina – and hopped to his home by the stream.

"Croak! Croak!" was all the toad's son said when he saw Thumbelina.

"Quiet!" said the old toad. "Don't wake her, or she might try to escape. We'll put her out in the stream on one of the big waterlily leaves. She's so small it will be like an island to her, and she won't be able to escape."

When Thumbelina awoke and found herself in the middle of the stream she started to cry.

The old toad swam out and spoke to her. "You will marry my son," he told Thumbelina, "and live with us in the mud. I'll come back for you when your new home is ready."

When the old toad had gone the fish who lived in the stream poked their heads out of the water to see the toad's bride. They saw the little girl weeping, and decided to help her.

They gnawed and gnawed at the

stalk of the waterlily leaf until it floated off down the stream, and soon Thumbelina was far, far away, where the toad could not follow.

Suddenly a big cockchafer beetle flew along and clasped Thumbelina in his claws. He flew to a tall tree and put Thumbelina down on a large leaf, and told her she was pretty. "Though you don't look anything like a cockchafer," he added.

Soon all the other beetles came to look at Thumbelina. "But she only has two legs – and no feelers!" said the beetles. "She looks quite human. Ugh!"

Even though the cockchafer still thought her pretty, he decided that he didn't want her anymore, and he carried her down from the tree.

Thumbelina lived alone in the forest through the summer. She wove blades of grass into a bed, and hung it from a large leaf like a hammock. She drank dew from the plants, and ate pollen from the flowers.

But then came the winter. The birds all flew away, the trees lost their leaves, and the flowers withered and died. When snowflakes started to fall Thumbelina shivered and wrapped a dead leaf around her shoulders; but it gave no warmth, and she decided to leave the forest to seek shelter.

She walked and walked until she reached a corn field on the edge of the forest. Only the dry stalks of the corn stood in the frozen ground, but it was like a wood to tiny Thumbelina.

At last she came to a small door among the stubble where a fieldmouse lived. She knocked on the door and asked if she could have a piece of corn to eat, and the kind old fieldmouse took her into her warm, dry kitchen, and fed Thumbelina until she could eat no more.

When she heard Thumbelina's story she shook her head sadly. "You may stay with me for the winter," said the old fieldmouse. "All I ask is that you keep my home neat and tidy, and tell me stories."

So Thumbelina and the fieldmouse lived happily together until one day a visitor arrived. "He has a fine home, and wears a rich velvet coat," said the fieldmouse. "He would make a fine husband for you."

But the visitor was a mole, and Thumbelina did not care for him, though he loved her singing. Before he left he took Thumbelina and the fieldmouse along a passage he had dug to connect the two houses. He wanted to show them a dead bird he had found there, a beautiful swallow.

That night Thumbelina could not stop thinking of the poor swallow, and she climbed from her bed and wove a warm coverlet of straw which she laid over the still bird. Then she laid her head against the bird's heart – and jumped back at once, for the bird had moved! The bird was not dead, but numbed by the cold, and the straw coverlet had warmed him so that his heart had started to beat again.

Thumbelina was very frightened, for the swallow was very much bigger than she was, but she decided to nurse him. So she went every night, when the fieldmouse was asleep, to feed and warm him.

Soon the swallow was able to speak. "Thank you for helping me," he said. "Soon I shall be strong again, and able to fly in the sun."

So the swallow stayed in the passage right through the winter, and when spring came round again he was fit and well. "I must go now," said the swallow, pecking his way out of the mole's tunnel. "Will you come with me?"

"I cannot," Thumbelina replied, "for the fieldmouse would be upset."

"Goodbye then," said the swallow, and Thumbelina watched sadly as he flew away.

Soon the corn started to grow, and Thumbelina was sad, for she was not allowed to leave the fieldmouse's house to catch a glimpse of the sky. She was even more sad when the fieldmouse told her that she was to marry the mole that autumn. She cried and cried, but the fieldmouse would not change her mind. "Think of the mole's well-stocked larder!" she scolded. "You're lucky to be marrying such a gentleman!"

On the day of the wedding Thumbelina stood at the door of the fieldmouse's home. "Farewell, bright sun!" she said. "I will not see you again, for I must live under the ground from now on. Farewell – and if ever you see the swallow, tell him I will always remember him."

At that moment she heard sweet birdsong overhead. It was the swallow! Thumbelina cried as she told him that she was to marry the mole, and he comforted her. "Winter is coming again," he said. "I am going to fly far away to a warm country. Come with me."

This time Thumbelina did not refuse. She clambered up onto the swallow's back. Soon they were flying high in the sky, over field and forest, lake and sea.

At last the swallow reached his home – a beautiful palace beside a huge lake. At the top of a tall white marble pillar sat the swallow's nest. "This is my home," said the swallow, "but I think you will be happier living in one of the flowers below."

On the green grass lay one of the tall marble pillars, broken into three pieces. Between the marble pieces grew tall white flowers, and it was to one of these that the swallow carried Thumbelina.

And what do you think she found there? A little prince, with tiny wings on his shoulders, and a shining gold crown on his head. He was the guardian of the flower, and no bigger than Thumbelina herself.

"How beautiful he is!" Thumbelina

whispered to the swallow, and the flower prince thought his unexpected visitor the prettiest thing he had ever seen. Right away he asked her what her name was, and if she would be his wife!

This was a man she could love – not like the toad or the mole – and so Thumbelina accepted.

From every flower came a tiny creature, and each one brought a present for their new princess. Best of all the gifts was a pair of wings. With them Thumbelina could fly from flower to flower; she could even visit the swallow in his nest.

After the wedding the prince turned to his bride. "Thumbelina is not a pretty enough name for you," he said. "From now on I will call you Maia."

When it was time for the swallow to leave the warm lands again he bade farewell to the prince and princess of the flowers and flew to a faraway land. There he made a nest over the window of a man who wrote fairytales. "Listen! Listen!" the swallow sang – and that is how we came to know his story.

The Nightingale

Long ago, in China, there lived a great and powerful emperor. He lived in a wonderful palace that was made entirely of rare porcelain that was so fragile that people had to move around very carefully for fear of breaking it. The palace's beauty was mirrored in a great lake that surrounded it, and in the garden were rare flowers, the most beautiful of which had bells that rang out whenever anyone passed nearby. The gardens stretched so far that even the gardener had no idea where they ended.

Beyond the gardens rose the tall trees of a dense forest, and it was through this forest that visitors came to marvel and wonder at the emperor's palace. When they returned home they wrote of the palace and the gardens – and the emperor was delighted to read their words.

But in every book that the emperor read, one sentence was the same: "But the nightingale is the best of all."

"Where is this bird, this nightingale?" the emperor asked. "I never knew such a bird existed in my kingdom, yet it appears I have one in my garden."

"Well," said the prime minister, "I've never heard of a nightingale."

"It's a disgrace that the whole world knows about the nightingale, yet I've never seen her," said the emperor. "I want her brought to me – tonight!"

The prime minister ran from room to room in the palace, but no one had seen or even heard of the nightingale. At last he came to the palace kitchens where a young maid was working. "Have you ever heard of the nightingale?" the prime minister asked for the hundredth time.

"The nightingale?" the young girl asked. "Of course I know it. How she can sing! When I visit my mother, who lives on the other side of the forest, I sometimes stop among the trees for a while just to hear her song. It's such a sad and lovely song that it brings tears of happiness to my eyes."

The prime minister smiled. "If you lead us to the nightingale you will be well rewarded," he said. "The emperor wants to hear the bird sing."

So the prime minister, the kitchen maid and many courtiers set out for the forest where the nightingale usually sang.

As they walked along a cow began to moo and prime minister stopped to listen. "I can hear it – but what a loud voice for a small bird."

"That's not the nightingale, but a cow mooing," said the kitchen maid.

Beside a pond they heard some frogs croaking. "What a lovely song," said one of the courtiers.

"That is just frogs croaking," said the kitchen maid, "but I think we will hear the nightingale soon."

She was right. "Look! There she is!" said the kitchen maid, pointing to a small bird in a tree close by.

"She looks a very dull bird," said one of the courtiers, but he stood entranced when she started to sing.

The prime minister stepped forward. "Most excellent nightingale," he said, "I have the honour to summon you to court this evening. The emperor wishes to hear you sing."

"My song sounds best here in the darkness among the tall trees of the forest," the nightingale replied, "but I will come."

That evening a great feast was held at the emperor's palace. On a golden perch beside the emperor's throne sat the nightingale, and at his command the bird sang more sweetly than she had ever done before. So beautifully that tears ran down the emperor's cheeks as he listened.

When the song had finished the emperor asked the nightingale what she wanted as reward. "Your tears are my reward," the little bird replied. "An emperor's tears have a strange power. I have had pay enough."

One day a parcel arrived at the palace. On it was written one word: NIGHTINGALE. Inside was a little toy, a clockwork nightingale. It was shaped like the real one, but studded with diamonds, rubies and sapphires. "Let the birds sing together," the emperor commanded, but the duet was not a success, for the real nightingale sang as the mood took her while the toy one sang notes over and over again.

"Dear nightingale, you shall live with me always," said the emperor, and it was so. The bird lived in a golden cage, but she was allowed to fly outside the palace twice during the day and once at night. Twelve footmen accompanied her, and each held a silk ribbon tied to her leg, so her outings were not happy ones.

Everyone liked the toy, and the clockwork bird was wound up time and time again, but the emperor tired of the tune and looked for the real nightingale.

Where was the nightingale? She had flown out of an open window, and no one had noticed.

"Ungrateful creature!" said the prime minister. "But it doesn't matter – the jewelled bird is better by far."

The next day all the emperor's subjects were invited to hear the mechanical bird sing, and they all marvelled at the sound – all except one man, who had heard the *real* nightingale. "The song is sweet," he said. "But there is something missing..."

The mechanical bird was placed on a special velvet cushion beside the emperor's bed, and for a year everyone listened to its song until they knew every trill and cluck by heart. Then one evening the bird gave a *whirr,*

whiz, snap, and the song ended.

The emperor sent for his doctor, but he could not mend the toy.

The royal clockmaker was more hopeful. "I can fix it," he said, "but the works are almost worn out. From now on the bird must only sing on very special occasions."

So the bird sang just once every

year, when the whole court would gather to hear it.

Five years later a great sadness swept over the land. The emperor was ill, and the royal doctor reported that he was unlikely to live much longer.

As the emperor lay in his bed Death hovered over him, taunting him with memories and regrets. "Do you remember? Do you remember?" Death taunted, until the emperor could bear it no longer.

"Music! Let me have music!" begged the emperor, turning to the mechanical bird which stood beside his bed. "Sing, golden bird, sing to drown the voice of Death." But the toy bird was silent; there was no one to wind it up.

Then all at once, a beautiful song rang out. Hearing of the emperor's illness the real nightingale had flown to the palace to sing for him.

"Sing on, little nightingale, sing on," whispered the emperor as Death, defeated by the joyful song of hope, retreated, and the emperor fell into a deep, refreshing sleep.

He awoke to find the nightingale still perched on a branch just outside his window. "How can I repay you?" he asked the bird.

"You have done so already," said the nightingale. "My reward is the tears of joy you shed when first you heard me sing."

"Stay with me always," begged the emperor, "and sing only when you wish. I will break the mechanical bird into a thousand pieces."

"Don't do that," said the nightingale. "It has done all it was asked to do,

and can do no more. As for me, I cannot make my home in a palace in a golden cage, but I'll come in the still of the evening and sing to you. I'll tell you of sadness and joy in your kingdom, of good and evil, for a bird sees many things that are hidden from an emperor's eyes. All I ask is that you keep our friendship secret."

The emperor promised that he would not reveal the secret, and the nightingale flew off.

Shortly after, when the servants came to attend to the emperor, who they thought was dying, they were surprised to find him standing in front of the window, dressed in his royal robes.

"Good morning," was all the emperor said.

The Wild Swans

Far away there lived a king who had eleven sons and one daughter. They had the best of everything: fine clothes, beautiful toys, and picture books that were hand-painted.

But their happy days were soon over, for their mother died, and almost immediately their father married again. His new wife hated the children from the moment she saw them, and banished them to the nursery, not allowing them to speak to their father.

Even though she no longer saw the princes, the new queen – who was really a witch – wanted to be rid of them forever, so she changed them into swans. "Fly away and never return," she told the eleven white birds. "No one will know what has become of you."

Princess Elise still lived at the palace – but not for long. The queen took her to live with a poor peasant couple, and told the king that his daughter had run away.

The young princess suffered many hardships in the years that followed, but she grew kinder and more beautiful as the years passed, and she never forgot her brothers.

One day, when she was fifteen, she decided to set out to find them. She had walked far from her home when she met an old woman. "I am searching for my eleven brothers," said Elise. "They are princes, and wear gold crowns on their heads. Have you seen them?"

"No, I haven't seen them," the old woman replied. "But yesterday I saw eleven white swans swimming in the river. They wore gold crowns."

Elise followed the river's course until she came to the great ocean. She could not see the swans, but she found eleven slim white feathers lying amongst the seaweed at the water's edge, so she knew they had been there. She sat down to wait for them.

As the sun was setting Elise saw eleven great white birds flying towards the shore, gold crowns on their heads. As the sun dipped below the horizon an amazing thing happened – the white swans disappeared, and in their place stood eleven princes. Elise recognised her brothers and ran towards them, calling their names.

Later, her eldest brother told Elise of the spell they lived under. "While the sun is above the horizon we fly about as swans," he explained, "but when the sun sets we regain our human forms. We must always be certain to have a safe place to land at sunset, for if we were flying when the sun sets, we would fall to our deaths."

"Do you live here by the shore?" asked Elise.

"No, we live far away," her brother replied. "We are allowed to visit our homeland only once a year, for eleven days. We have just two days left, then we must fly away."

"But you must take me with you!" said Elise. "I cannot lose you again!"

At daybreak the swans flew away from the shore, only returning at nightfall. "We will make a net of willow bark and reeds so that we can carry you with us," the eldest prince told Elise, and they worked through the night to finish the strong net.

At daybreak the princes turned into swans again, and they seized the net in their beaks and flew off, so that Elise was borne high over the waves. All through the day they flew, until at last, as the sun began to set, they glimpsed a tiny rock that jutted from the sea. "We must reach the rock before the sun sets," one of the swans told Elise. "It is our only chance of safety."

With seconds to spare the swans landed on the rock and took on their human forms. The rock was hardly big enough to hold all twelve of them, but they clug to it right through the

night, as huge waves battered against them.

As soon as it was light the swans picked up the net and flew away from the rock until they reached the land where they lived. It was a land of green forests and flower-strewn meadows, and Elise thought it the most beautiful place she had ever seen.

As the sun began to sink below the horizon the swans stopped outside a deep cave whose mouth was almost covered by trailing plants. "Rest here," said the princes.

At once Elise fell asleep, and in her dreams she met the old woman again. "I have come to tell you how you may free your brothers from the spell they are under," the old woman said. "This is what you must do. Around the cave and in the nearby churchyard grow stinging nettles. You must gather them, even though their stings blister your hands, then crush them with your bare feet. From the yarn they yield you must weave eleven shirts with long sleeves. When you throw

the shirts over the swans, the spell will be broken. But there is something you must remember: from the moment you start gathering the nettles until the moment you finish weaving, you must not speak. If you make a sound, or write a single word, your brothers will die! Their lives depend on your silence . . ."

As soon as she awoke Elise set out in search of the graveyard where the nettles grew. There, despite the pain, she gathered stinging nettles all day long, then trod them into flax before returning to the cave.

When her brothers returned at sunset they asked what she was weaving, but of course Elise would not utter a sound.

It was the youngest prince who saw Elise's blistered hands. "Look at her hands!" he cried. "Whatever she is doing, she is doing for us, I am sure!"

Tears fell from his eyes, and as the moisture touched the blisters they disappeared, so that Elise felt no more pain. She smiled her thanks.

From then on Elise worked day and

night, finishing one shirt after another. But on the third day, as she sat spinning, Elise heard the sound of a hunting horn, and the baying of hounds.

Nearer and nearer they came, until the hounds rushed into the cave, followed by the huntsmen. "Why are you here, child?" asked one of the huntsmen, who was king of the land.

Elise only shook her head, not daring to speak.

"This is no place for a beautiful young girl," said the king, pulling Elise to her feet and sitting her on his horse. "Come with me to my castle. I will look after you." And, despite Elise's desperate struggles, he rode off with her.

Elise lived in great luxury at the castle, and was dressed in fine silks and jewels, but she was unhappy.

Even when the king called his people together and told them that he had chosen Elise as his bride she wept silently. "There's something odd about a girl who cries at her engagement," said the old

archbishop, who wanted the king to marry his niece. "I think she's a witch."

The king took no notice of the old man's words, but he was concerned about Elise's unhappiness. "Look what I have had made for you," he said one day. "It is a room made to look like the cave I found you in. Here are your nettles, and your shirts. Perhaps now you'll be happy."

Elise smiled for the first time and kissed the king's hand in thanks.

Every night, when the castle slept, Elise went to the little room and continued her task, but when she had finished six shirts she had no more nettles. Quietly she left the castle and travelled back to the churchyard to gather more, ignoring the witches who sat among the tombstones.

But the archbishop had seen her, and he spoke to the king. "She's a witch, I tell you. I saw her there with the other evil witches," he said. "You must be rid of her."

The king didn't want to believe the archbishop, but the old man was so insistent that he agreed to follow the girl that night.

By now Elise had only one more shirt to weave, and she set off to the churchyard for the last time.

The king and the archbishop watched as she disappeared behind a gravestone – and then gasped as they saw the old witches sitting there in the gloom. The king hid his face, for he thought Elise was one of them.

"The people shall judge her," he said . . . and the people condemned Elise to be burned.

The king himself rode with Elise to the prison, all the time begging her to speak in her own defence. But she would not.

Guards threw her into a dirty cell, and threw the nettles and shirts in after her. "Here, make your bed on those," they laughed.

There was no gift Elise would rather have had, and she worked on, hoping that she would be spared long enough to finish the eleven shirts that would free her brothers.

Some days later great crowds gathered in the streets, for this was the day the witch was to be burned. Even in the rough cart that took her to the

place of execution Elise worked on. Ten finished shirts lay at her feet, and the eleventh was ready, apart from one last sleeve.

Suddenly eleven great white swans swooped down and landed on the cart, and Elise threw the shirts over them. One by one the swans changed into young men . . . until only the youngest remained. With a sad sigh Elise threw the almost-finished shirt over him, and he too became a young man – but where his left arm should have been there was a swan's wing!

Elise hugged her brothers. "I can speak at last!" she cried. "The spell is broken, and you are safe!"

But such was her relief and joy that she could not find words to tell her story, and it was left to her brothers to explain. "She is innocent, your majesty," the eldest began. "Her suffering and silence was for us. She has freed us from a wicked spell."

The youngest prince took up the story. "To set us free she had to weave nettle-hair shirts for us – and she had to do it in silence. She is no witch, sire."

As he finished speaking the sweet scent of roses filled the air. Every twig

around the stake where Elise was to have been burned had burst into flower!

The king knelt at Elise's feet and begged her to forgive him – and to be his bride. Now able to speak at last, she agreed, and Elise and the king, with her eleven brothers, made their way back to the castle.

There, amid great rejoicing, they were married. And the only reminder of their strange adventure was the winged arm of the youngest prince . . .

The Princess and the Pea

In a far off land there once lived a prince who wished to marry a princess. It was very important to him that the girl should be a *real* princess.

He travelled all over the world in search of a bride, but there was something wrong with every princess that he met. There was always something about the princesses that didn't appear to be quite as it should; he could never be sure that they were genuine princesses.

So after many months of searching the prince travelled home again, still without a bride.

One evening there was a terrible storm. Thunder raged until it rattled the windows, lightning flashed across the sky, and the rain fell as though it would never stop.

In the midst of the terrible storm there came a quiet knock on the palace door, and the old king went to see who was there.

Standing in the rain he found a girl who said she was a princess, and who begged shelter. She didn't look much like a princess, for the rain ran down her hair and over her clothes, and streamed out through the tips of her shoes. But she said she was a real princess, so the king asked her inside.

I'll soon find out if she's a real princess, the old queen thought, and without saying a word she went into the spare bedroom.

She took off all the bedclothes, and laid a tiny pea on the bed. On top of the pea she piled twenty thick mattresses, and on top of the mattresses she piled twenty feather quilts.

The queen showed the princess into the bedroom. "You may stay here tonight," she said. "Sleep well."

In the morning the queen asked the girl if she had slept well.

"It was awful," said the girl. "I didn't get a wink of sleep all night. Heaven knows what was in the bed, but I lay on a huge hard thing that has made me black and blue with bruises. It was dreadful."

The queen smiled. She was sure that this girl really was a princess. Who but a real princess could have felt the tiny pea through twenty thick mattresses and twenty feather quilts?

So the prince married his real princess – and the tiny pea was placed in the royal museum. Perhaps it's still there today...

The Ugly Duckling

It was summer in the country. The corn was yellow, the oats were ripe, and haystacks stood in every field.

In the tall reeds by a still lake a duck sat on her nest, waiting for her eggs to hatch. One by one the eggs began to crack, and one by one yellow ducklings appeared.

When they had all hatched out the mother duck sat beside the reeds. "Good," she said, "all hatched safely."

Then she noticed that one egg was still in the nest. It was the biggest egg, and it wasn't even cracked. Wearily she sat on the egg again and, at last, after a couple of hours it started to crack. But Mother Duck got an unpleasant surprise when the last of her offspring poked his head from the shell. He was nothing like her other fluffy ducklings! He was big and quite ugly!

"What an ugly duckling!" said a

very old duck who passed by the nest. "That's not a duck at all – it's a turkey! The lady from the farm must have slipped it into your nest. Turkeys mean trouble. I'd turn it out of the nest if I were you."

But Mother Duck felt sorry for the poor ugly grey duckling, and decided to let it stay.

The next day Mother Duck led her ducklings down to the edge of the lake. She was going to teach them how to swim.

Mother Duck swam across the lake, and one by one the ducklings

followed her. They all swam well, and the ugly grey duckling was the best swimmer by far. "He's no turkey," said Mother Duck. "Look how well he swims!"

After their swimming lesson Mother Duck led her ducklings into the farmyard to introduce them to all the other birds. The older ducks clucked over the new ducklings – but when they saw the grey duckling they backed away. "How ugly he is!" said one old

duck. "Take him away! We don't want *him* in the farmyard."

"But he hasn't done any harm," said Mother Duck, fluffing out his grey down. "And perhaps he'll grow less ugly in time."

But the little grey duckling didn't grow any prettier, and he had a very unhappy time in the farmyard. The ducks and hens snapped at him, and the girl who fed the birds pushed him to one side with her foot. In time even his brothers and sisters made fun of him, and wouldn't let him join in their games. "Go away, you ugly thing," they said. "We won't play with you."

Even Mother Duck was ashamed of her duckling, and began to think she would be better off without him. She started to pick on him, too.

The ugly duckling was very unhappy, and one night he decided to run away.

"Where are you going?" asked an owl.

"I'm going to find a place to live where people will like me, and not call me ugly," said the duckling.

"Good luck," said the owl. "You'll need it, for you really are the ugliest bird I've ever seen."

At last the ugly duckling reached the marshes where the wild ducks lived. They didn't know what to make of him, but at least they didn't drive him away. "You can stay here as long as you don't try to marry into the family," they told him. "Just keep out of our way."

The ugly duckling did just that, for all he wanted was a place to rest and water to drink.

After a couple of days two wild goslings flew to the marsh. "Hello," said the goslings. "Why not come with us to another marsh? You're so ugly that we quite like you. Come on."

At that moment loud bangs rang out over the marsh, and the two goslings fell down dead! There was a shoot going on, and hunters with guns surrounded the marsh, shooting at the ducks and geese.

The ugly duckling hid his head under his wing. He was terrified, and he started to tremble as a large gun dog splashed through the reeds towards him. The dog saw him, and thrust his muzzle at him, but then splashed on in search of bigger game.

"Thank goodness," said the ugly duckling. "I'm so ugly that even the gun dog won't come near me."

It was many hours before the ugly duckling dared to move, but at last, when the shooting had stopped and the marsh was still and quiet again, he hurried away.

The ugly duckling walked across many fields and meadows until he was far away from the marsh. In the corner of a field he saw a tumbledown cottage whose front door hung crookedly from a broken hinge, and he slipped through the gap and into a warm kitchen.

In the cottage lived an old woman with her cat and hen. When they noticed the ugly duckling the cat began to purr and the hen to cluck.

"What's this?" said the old woman, peering at the ugly duckling. Her eyesight was poor, and she mistook the young bird for a plump duck. "What luck! Now I'll have duck eggs for breakfast!"

So the old woman gave the ugly duckling a home, but it was not a happy one.

"Can you lay eggs?" the hen asked, and tossed her head when the ugly duckling replied that he could not.

"Can you arch your back and

purr?'' asked the cat, and turned his back when the ugly duckling shook his head. ''You're a useless creature, then,'' he added.

The ugly duckling decided that he would have to leave, and the next morning he did just that.

He spent the summer months swimming on the lakes and marshes, moving from place to place in search of friends and a home, but he didn't find them.

Soon autumn came, and the skies were grey and dark. Strong winds blew the leaves from the trees, and soon winter's icy breath was in the air.

It was so cold that the ugly duckling had to keep swimming round and round to stop the water freezing into ice, but every night the circle he swam in grew smaller and smaller, until one morning a passing farmer found the duckling frozen fast in the ice, lifeless.

The farmer carried the duckling home, and he soon revived in the warm kitchen. The farmer's children were thrilled with their new pet, and they rushed over to play with him, arms outstretched.

But the poor ugly duckling thought they were going to harm him, and he

flew off in fright – knocking over a tall jug of milk. The farmer's wife shrieked, the children laughed – and the ugly duckling flew into the butter tub, then fluttered through the flour barrel! What a mess he was – and how frightened! He flew out through the open door, and didn't stop to rest until he was far, far away.

That winter was a hard one for the young bird. Snow lay thick on the ground, the wind howled through the trees, and he found little food and poor shelter among the bare bushes.

But one day as he huddled in the reed beds he heard a bird start to sing, and felt weak rays of sunlight on his feathers. Spring had come at last!

The duckling raised his wings. They seemed much stronger than before, and carried him easily into the air, high over the marsh. Almost before he knew it he found himself in a large garden full of budding fruit trees and green lawns. On a lake below him swam three beautiful white swans, and when he saw them a strange sadness came over him.

"I will fly down to those beautiful birds," he decided. "They will surely peck me to death for daring to come near them, but I don't care. What future is there for an ugly creature like me? Better to die than to spend another hard winter with no friends."

The young bird felt shy, and hid his head under his wing. Yet he was not proud, for he remembered how he had been scorned, before he turned from an ugly duckling into a beautiful swan. He knew that pride was a foolish thing.

At last he raised his head, and gazed around at his new home. He ruffled his feathers happily and swam round and round the lake. It was the start of a happy life for the ugly duckling – who was now a beautiful swan.

The swans swam towards the young bird as soon as they saw him, and he bowed his head. "Yes, kill me," said the ugly duckling.

But what did he see reflected in the water? Not his ugly grey shape, but beautiful white feathers, a long yellow beak, and a graceful arched neck. He was a swan!

The three swans swam around him in welcome, and some children ran to the side of the lake. "Look, there's a new swan on the lake," one of the children cried. "And he's the most beautiful of all! Look how handsome he is!"

The Little Match Girl

It was the last day of the old year. Light spilled from every window in the town as people gathered to bid goodbye to the old year and welcome to the new. The sounds of cheerful laughter and music filled the air and sometimes, through an uncurtained window, passers by glimpsed gaily-dressed ladies, and tables laden with fine china and silverware. The tables groaned under the weight of joints of meat, savouries and rich desserts.

Outside, the streets were still and quiet, the only sound to be heard was the crunch of snow as a late guest hurried on his way. It was bitterly cold, and snowflakes fell steadily.

Through the deserted streets a

lonely, frail figure moved. It was a young girl, dressed in tattered rags. Snowflakes clung to her hair, and she was very cold and hungry.

All day long she had walked through the city streets, barefoot, her hands blue with cold. She clutched small bundles of matches which she had been trying to sell. But no one had wanted to buy matches, and now, as the streets became more and more deserted, she realised that there would be no customers.

Though she could hardly walk with cold and exhaustion, the little match girl dared not return to her home. She knew that she would be beaten if she returned with unsold matches.

Eventually the little match girl had to rest, and she sat down in a corner where two houses met, drawing her feet under her for warmth, and rubbing her cold hands. She dropped the bundles of matches to the ground when a thought struck her. The light of even one match might warm her cramped fingers, so she struck a match on the wall.

It flared with a bright light, and the girl looked deep into the flame. As she looked she saw a firelit room, with blazing logs burning in the hearth. She could almost feel the heat of the fire warming her frozen body.

But in a second the match's flame flickered and died, and the little girl was back in the cold street.

She lit another match, and now, as she looked into its flame, she was back in the firelit room, this time standing by a table laden with meats and fruits. She stretched out her hand towards the food . . . but as she did so the flame flickered and died.

The light from the third match revealed a tall Christmas tree. The green branches were laden with golden balls and gaily-wrapped parcels, and on the end of each branch flickered a tiny candle. The little match girl stretched out her hand to touch the tree. . . but as she did so the match went out, and the tree disappeared.

As the little match girl looked up into the dark night sky, one of the stars fell, the light streaming behind it like a fiery tail. The little girl sighed sadly. "Somewhere, someone is dying," she whispered.

Her grandmother, who had died some years before but who was remembered by the little girl as being kind and gentle, had told her that whenever a star fell from the sky it meant that someone had died. The match girl had never forgotten her grandmother's words.

She struck another match, and this time in its flame she saw her grandmother, smiling kindly as she always had. "Don't leave me when the flame dies, Grandmother!" the match girl pleaded. "Stay with me, for I am cold and lonely."

As the flame flickered she lit match after match, so that the image of her grandmother would not disappear.

From the pool of light that glowed around her, Grandmother grasped her cold, numbed fingers, and pulled the little girl into the sky. They didn't stop until they were high above the clouds, in a safe place where neither hunger nor cold would ever trouble the little match girl again.

As her frail body disappeared into the heavens, the bells of the city rang out. They rang farewell to the old year, and welcome to the new year.

In the cold morning of New Year's Day the body of the little match girl was found, huddled between two houses. Around her were her unsold matches, and the spent matches lay here and there, black against the white snow.

"Poor child, she was trying to warm herself with matches!" the people who found her said. "Poor little match girl."

But they were puzzled by the happy smile on her lips. How could they know that she had gone to a happier place?